A TALE OF TWO VICTORIA CROSSES

Lieutenant General (Retd) Baljit Singh

PENTAGON PRESS

A TALE OF TWO VICTORIA CROSSES

Lieutenant General (Retd) Baljit Singh

ISBN 978-81-8274-885-9

First Published in 2017

Published by
PENTAGON PRESS
206, Peacock Lane, Shahpur Jat,
New Delhi-110049
Phones: 011-64706243, 26491568
Telefax: 011-26490600
email: rajan@pentagonpress.in
website: www.pentagonpress.in

Printed at Aegean Offset Printers, Greater Noida, U.P.

To the Memory of
Lieutenant Karamjeet Singh Judge,
VICTORIA CROSS (Posthumous),
March 18, 1945.

CONTENTS

ACKNOWLEDGMENTS

Many friends have been generous both with their time and patience in meeting my demands for related military history background, validation checks and more crucially, for providing connected images. Squadron Leader (Retired) RTS Chhina (Secretary, Centre For Armed Forces Historical Research, USI of India, New Delhi) always had an answer for my nagging doubts and for pictures of Regimental insignia (past & present) of the Sikh and Punjab Regiments; and of 15 Ludhiana Sikhs arrival in France for WW I, an artist's recreation of one of their heroic combat actions and the fetching portrait of Lieutenant JG Smyth wearing the VC medal-ribbon. And above all, for researching the site (together with a photograph) of the Tankkyan Cremation Memorial (Mayanmar) where the last rites of Lieutenant Karamjeet Singh Judge were performed, in the midst of the war in March, 1945.

Colonel Rohit Gupta had commanded his Sapper Regiment two years ago in the Infantry Division which was raised by and led to war in Burma by Major General JG Smyth, VC, MC, and in the process, collected Smyth memorabilia; he readily provided pictures of Smyth from childhood, as Gentleman Cadet at Sandhurst (UK) and from Smyth's time at the Defence Services Staff College, Camberley (UK), from Smyth's book, Milestones.

But the largest and intimate inputs of Karamjeet and his kin are a priceless gift from Ms Shah-E-Naaz J Kohli (Boogie) and I simply lack words to thank her adequately. Admittedly, it was her dad who had triggered this "Tale" but without the photographs she searched assiduously, this book would have lacked much of its credibility, purpose and charm.

Major General Dhruv C Katoch, SM, VSM (Retd) has been magnanimous with time and editorial advice which immensely enhanced the readability of the book. Not just that but the General also volunteered to format the text and images which a publisher without military background would scarcely have managed, quite as well.

As always, my wife's encouragements and forbearance were the utmost motivation to piece together the text and fulfil this pending desire of mine.

PROLOGUE

"Every man gives his life for what he believes. Every woman gives her life for what she believes. Some people believe in little or nothing, nevertheless they give up their lives for that little or nothing. One life is all we have. And we live it as we live it, and believe in living it, and then it is gone. But to surrender what you are, and to live without belief – that is more terrible than dying – more terrible than dying young."

—Anonymous.

This is a tale of two intensely pitched combat actions, led by two subalterns in the service of the British Indian Army, one a Briton and the other an Indian of almost the same age, and fought against two different foes but on two battle fields, on two continents separated by oceans and thirty years in time. Both Subalterns would be awarded the Victoria Cross "FOR VALOUR" and in a strange coincidence the Briton would become the iconic inspiration for the Indian and ultimately, the courage of one would match the others' identically in the manner possible only among biological, zygotic twins!

The moment of the Indian lad's inspiration had come in a flash when walking to college in the company of his elder brother, they came across a hoarding put out over night in Jullundur town of Punjab Province, urging Indians to recruit in the Indian Army for the Allies war against the Axis Powers, in 1939. On the upper half of that hoarding was an attractive portrait of the handsome Lieutenant John Smyth of the 15th Ludhiana Sikhs, proudly wearing his VC medal, awarded for taking up the gauntlet of a near suicidal mission in the Ypres salient in France, on May 18, 1915 during WW I. Both brothers stared at John Smyth's visage as though in a mesmeric trance till the younger said in all earnestness *"chalo, aapaan we ik ik Victoria Cross laekay iyea, prah Ji" (Let us go and get a VC each, brother).*

The brothers were the sons of Sardar Sunder Singh Judge, Inspector General Police of the Kapurthala princely state in Punjab. Ajit Singh being the elder declared that he would join the 15th Ludhiana Sikhs, come what may and so Karamjeet pitched in for the Punjab Regiment. Not trusting their chances of success with the entrance examination to the Indian Military Academy for a commission into the officer cadre, they opted for the alternate route of "Y Cadets", that is, a scheme aimed at encouraging educated youth from affluent families to enrol in the ranks for a start and a year later, seek nomination to join an OTS (Officer Training School) and ultimately become a commissioned officer.

FOR VALOUR

Captain John Smyth, VC, MC, 15th Ludhiana Sikhs.
Portrait by George Carr Drinkwater.

THE CATALYST VC WHICH INSPIRED ANOTHER SUBALTERN

LIEUTENANT JOHN SMYTH, VC

Of course, the poster had revealed to the brothers not a whit about Smyth's mission of May 18, 1915 leading to the VC, the essence of which is perhaps best recounted in a narrative from the publication, "Deeds That Thrill The Empire" (Hutchison & Co):

> *"There are no finer fighting men in our Indian Army than the Sikhs, the descendants of those fierce long-haired warriors who fought so stubbornly against us at Ferozshah and Chalianwala, and afterwards stood so loyally by the British Raj in the dark days of the mutiny. And there are no finer officers in the world than the men who lead them.... And on many a desperate enterprise, and many a forlorn hope, did these officers lead him, but surely on none more so than that on which Lieutenant Smyth, of the 15th Sikhs, led his little band of dark-skinned heroes on May 18th, 1915.... The names of these ten heroes*

deserve to be remembered. They were: Sepoys Fatteh Singh, Ganda Singh, Harnam Singh, Lal Singh, Naik Mangal Singh, Sarain Singh, Sapooram Singh, Sucha Singh, Sunder Singh, and Ujagar Singh".

That mission had involved ferrying ammunition replenishment to one beleaguered and isolated bunker over a distance of some 250 yards but the ground to be traversed was so exposed and dominated by German fire that two attempts by the Highland Light Infantry and another by the 15th Sikhs had failed to the last man, in each case. That was the stage when it fell to Smyth to lead another attempt. And when Smyth faced his battalion and asked for ten volunteers, such was their motivation that the entire lot stepped forward! Smyth was to confess that their spontaneity had "cured me of blue funk" and twenty minutes later…

"Before they advanced a score of yards on their terrible journey, Fatteh Singh fell, severely wounded; in another hundred, Sucha Singh, Ujagar Singh and Sunder Singh were down, leaving only Lieutenant Smyth and six men to get the ammunition boxes along. However, spurred on by the dire necessity of their comrades ahead, they, by super human efforts, succeeded in dragging them nearly to the end of the trench when, in quick succession, Sarain Singh, Harnam Singh and Sapooram Singh were shot dead, while Ganda Singh and Naik Mangal Singh were wounded. The second box of bombs had therefore to be abandoned, and for the two remaining men to haul even one box along in the face of such difficulties appeared an impossible task. But nothing was impossible for the young Lieutenant and the heroic Lal Singh,

and presently the anxious watchers in the trench ahead saw them wriggling their way yard by yard into the open, dragging with them the box upon the safe arrival of which so much depended.

As they emerged from the comparative shelter of the trench into the open, a veritable hail of lead burst upon them; but escaping it though by a miracle, they crawled on until they found themselves confronted by a small stream which at this point was too deep to wade... Across they struggled with their precious burden, the water all about them churned into foam by the storm of bullets, clambered up the further bank, and in a minute more they were among their cheering comrades. Both were unhurt though their clothes were perforated by bullet holes; but it is sad to relate that scarcely they had reached the trench that the gallant Lal Singh was struck by a bullet and killed instantly".

For this most "conspicuous bravery" Lieut Smyth received the Victoria Cross and each of the brave men who had accompanied him, the Indian Distinguished Service Medal, and we may be very certain that *"ne'er will their glory fade"* from the proud record of our Indian army".

Now post armistice, 15th Ludhiana Sikhs (presently 2 SIKH) were back to business as usual in the North West Frontier's Waziristan region. In the normal course, John Smyth guided a protective patrol to get up a spur from which they would ensure safe passage of the incoming logistics column. However the tribal snipers had their own game plan and Smyth who was in the lead, received a bullet through his left palm. Unmindful of the wound and resultant disability, he deployed the patrol team to keep up the engagement with the snipers while he slithered down and clawed up another spur and half an hour later, wielding rifle with one hand, both snipers were silenced for good. And four years to the day after his VC, Smyth would now be decorated by a Military Cross (MC)!

In July 1936 Major John Smyth was promoted to the rank of Lieutenant Colonel and given command of 45 Rattrays Sikhs (presently 3 SIKH), who were deployed in the Chitral Valley. But strange and often cruel are the ways of a soldier's destiny. Less than a decade later, Smyth, now promoted to the acting rank of Major General, was handpicked to lead the first Allied formation into Burma, intended to thwart the Japanese juggernaut. However, against his cool military judgement, his plan for defence of Burma was turned down by his superiors. In the event, a month down the timeline, he was constrained to order demolition of the only bridge over the River Sittang in the vicinity of Rangoon, despite a fairly large body of his Division being committed in a running battle with the enemy on the far bank and the Division was mauled.

Smyth had forewarned his Corps Commander of the adverse consequences of the defensive plan he was forced to adopt, and in the event, his crystal gazing proved to be tragically omniscient. Notwithstanding those warnings given well in time, the axe fell on Smyth. Prime Minister Winston Churchill and C-in-C India,

General APJ Wavell (both of whom were desperate for an Allied victory on any battlefield), summarily sacked Smyth from command and dismissed him from the Service. Going by military regulations, Smyth dropped to his substantive rank which at the time was, a Lieutenant Colonel. There was more humiliation in store as Smyth and his wife Frances, did not have enough credit in their bank to buy a sea passage home to London. A bigger personal blow came two years later. His elder son, successfully led his company (the company commander having been killed) during the final and successful assault on the Jail Hill Ridge at Kohima. Moments after achieving success, he fell prey to a Japanese sniper and was killed in action (KIA).

But Smyth was in the true mould of a sphinx; shortly he would emerge as the lead war correspondent of The Times, London as also much in demand by the BBC for broadcasts on the war in Europe. Once the Wimbledon Championships were revived, Smyth became the much applauded Chair Umpire cum Master of Ceremonies for two decades running, won election (twice) to the British Parliament and the doughty Sir Winston Churchill made him a Minister in his Cabinet, the Queen appointed him Founder Chairman of the VC Committee as also an Honorary Brigadier (Whitehall had refused to bend rules to re-instate him in his old rank). Smyth authored "History of Lawn Tennis" which was acknowledged a classic, but perhaps his happiest moment of a fulfilled lifetime arrived in 1959, playing proud host to the brass bands contingent from the

Indian Army performing for the annual Military Night Tattoo, Edinburgh! The Band-Major was a Sikh Naib Subedar and the Brass Band segment was also exclusively made up of Sikh soldiers. All of them were six foot something tall, broad shouldered, with rolled up black beards, be-medaled and resplendent in their colorful regimental uniforms. The percussionist had the extra swagger with a leopard skin draped over his upper torso. After the concluding night's performance, over the cobbled-stone forecourt inside the Edinburgh Castle, Smyth's comrades-in-arms of old would put aside their music instruments, and led by the straight-as-a-lance Sikh Subedar, they marched up to the front row of by now a hushed audience and lifting the ***"CO Sahib Bahadur"*** on their shoulders, dance a spirited jig and the mammoth audience spontaneously burst into a thunderous applause! Once they stood Smyth back on his feet, those plucky few would call out 'WAHAY GURU JI KA KHALSA, WAHAY GURU JI KI FATEH' and the audience would befittingly respond with a mother of all applauses.

It was my good fortune to witness this once in lifetime, soldierly bonhomie! In fact, it brought a flood of memories of my ancestral links with the Sikh Regiment. My maternal great grandfather, Subedar Kaka Singh had served in the 4th and 54th Sikh from February 1897 to 06 March, 1908 with distinction and the memorabilia traceable with his grandson is this letter, a kind of a testimonial:

"Subedar Kaka Singh, son of Bela Singh has served in the 4th and 54 Sikhs for upward of 25 years and has been a Native Officer in the Regiment since Feb 1897. He has served six times in expeditions (battles) on the NW Frontier. He served two years as Native Officer Instructor at the School of Musketry, Chaangla Gali. He is very smart, energetic and an intelligent officer. He has applied to go on pension because his wife is very ill and he must give up his time to her.

I consider him an exceptionally able officer and hope he will obtain some good appointment near his home.

Sd:
Kenneth Buchanan
Lt Col
Comdg 54 Sikh PF
06.01.1908"

When Kaka Singh's younger son, Partap Singh (my maternal grandfather) turned sixteen, he was promptly enrolled in 15th Ludhiana Sikhs. Whenever in my childhood we went visiting him, he would regale me with stories from India's North West Frontier (present day Baluchistan and Eastwards up to the Khyber-Pakhtunkhwa regions of Pakistan), especially of the courage and the unlimited fighting perseverance of the Afghan tribes. And if it was a summers day, he would have his cot laid out under the shade of a Neem tree (there being no electricity in those days), and strip down to the traditional Sikh shorts to beat the summer heat. And I would hold him in awe and admiration because he carried the scar of a bullet on his right breast and two huge scars on his left thigh, the result of a bullet's entry and exit. He was invalided on medical grounds but was proud to receive his paltry pension (pronounced by all pensioners of yore in Punjab as "Pillsun") which in today's monetary scales will be no more than one hundred rupees! But for them the "Pillsun" was the talisman of honour; nothing more and nothing less.

Smyth as "Cabin Boy on the Blue Dragon, 1907".

Gentleman Cadet JG Smyth at Sandhurst, 1911; inset "My Subedar Major Kaka Singh Bahadur OBI, IDSM at Coronation in London 1937".

Smyth at home after the VC Investiture.

Lieut Smyth leads; only six survive of the eleven who had set out twenty minutes earlier.

Of the team of eleven, only Smyth and Sepoy Lal Singh survive at this moment; they carry one ammunition box, but a moment later 'Lal Singh was struck by a bullet & killed instantly'.

"A Point-to-Point in 1924 at Staff College, Camberley"
[Smyth astride Skylark, riding farther horse]

Lieut John Smyth (3rd from Right edge of photo frame) in the midst of his 15th Ludhiana Sikhs, in France.

JG Smyth, VC, MC in full dress uniform, presumably as *Commanding Officer, 45 Rattrays Sikhs.*

FOR VALOUR

Lieut Karamjeet Singh Judge, 4th Bn,15 Punjab Regiment, in 1943.

THIRTY YEARS APART AND SUPREMELY VALOROUS

LIEUT KARAMJEET SINGH JUDGE, VC (POSTHUMOUS)

Unfortunately for Cadet Ajit Singh Judge who as a "Y Cadet" had enrolled in 45 Rattrays Sikhs, he would be denied Commission into the Army's Sword Arm but instead allotted the Regiment of Artillery which in the event would place him at a great disadvantage in the two brothers quest for a VC, each. Cadet Karamjeet Singh Judge would, however, move closer to his dream when on May 30, 1943 he was commissioned into the 4th Battalion of 15 Punjab Regiment, which would be on the Order of Battle of General (later Field Marshal) Slim's, reconstituted Fourteenth Army. Thus, both brothers would have the honour to serve in the Indian Army, which for the first time in its long and chequered past went to war in defence of the motherland, against foreign aggression poised through Burma.

The Japanese final push to invade India was resolutely defeated by the Fourteenth Army in the twin battles fought concurrently at Kohima and Imphal, which since have been recognised as the two most decisive battles of WW II. And General Slim was now on the cusp to enter the Hall of Fame of celebrated Warlords of Military History when he decided to modify his earlier war plan by switching the weight of his counter offensive with an out flanking pincer by IV Corps, aimed at the capture of Meiktila (the single, largest logistics base of the Japanese in Burma) and thus trapping and destroying almost the entire Japanese army, engaged mostly around and north of Mandalay.

On 14 February, 1945 General Slim set IV Corps "to seize a bridgehead over the River Irrawaddy East of Pokokku" and follow through swiftly the capture of Meiktila, the jugular of the entire opposing Japanese Army in Burma. And shortly, 7 Infantry Division would lead the pincer, probe the West bank of the river for a suitable crossing and "the 4th, 15th Punjabis reinforced the first wave so that by nightfall of 23 February, 1945 a small bridgehead had been occupied. Slim ordered Messervy to pass 17 Infantry Division across the river in readiness for its drive on Meiktila... And by 27 February the "Black Cats" began to dash for Meiktila."

Thus, the Japanese were outwitted by General Slim and in the penultimate phase for the capture of Meiktila, the 4th Punjab Battalion supported by C Squadron of 116 Regiment (Gordon Highlanders) Royal Armoured

Corps, were tasked to capture the Cotton Mills Area in the vicinity of Myingyan port on the River Irrawaddy. During the second phase of that battle, when Lieutenant Karamjeet Singh with his platoon and a troop of tanks were in the process of clearing an unspecified number of fortified bunkers and how that combat unfolded, is best summed up by this extract from the London Gazette of 03 July 1945:

"4/15th were part of Lieut. Colonel Hubert Conroy's33 Brigade whose job was to clear the forest in a triangle around Nyaungyan bridgehead. South of Nyaungyan they attacked Sindewa, a heavily defended Japanese position in the jungle, thick with trees. There were extensive minefields.

On 18 March 1945 during the Battle of Meiktila in Burma (now Myanmar) he was ordered to capture a cotton mill. The assault began with an attack on the strategic river port of Myingyan. By all accounts, even before receiving the posthumous award, Lieut. Karamjeet Singh was a brave soldier. Always eager to engage in actions, he confided in his company commander, Major TM Whitmarsh-Knight, his desire for glory. The following morning, the Jat company comprising Indian soldiers was to spearhead the assault. They were supported by the Sherman tanks of No 2 Troop, C Squadron, 116 Regiment (Gordon Highlanders), Royal Armoured Corps, commanded by Lieut. Hugh Baker.

Karamjeet Singh was just 21 years old, and a Lieutenant in the 4th Battalion, 15 Punjab Regiment, in the British Indian Army during World War II when he performed the following deeds for which he was awarded the VC during the battle of

Myingyan which raged over four days; Baker exclaimed later that Karamjeet was the **"bravest soldier I have ever seen"***... Though facing stiff enemy resistance (a total of almost 200 enemy shells fell around the tanks and infantry during the attack) and in unsuitable terrain for tanks, he dominated the battlefield by his numerous and successive acts of superb gallantry; until he fell in the last stages of the action.*

The citation reads:

> *The KING has been graciously pleased to approve the posthumous award of the VICTORIA CROSS to:—*
>
> *Lieutenant Karamjeet Singh JUDGE (IEC. 5504), 15th Punjab Regiment, Indian Army.*
>
> *In Burma, on 18th March, 1945, C Company of the 15th Punjab Regiment, in which Lieutenant Karamjeet Singh Judge was a Platoon Commander, was ordered to capture the Cotton Mill area on the outskirts of Myingyan. In addition to numerous bunkers and stiff enemy resistance a total of almost 200 enemy shells fell around the tanks and infantry during the attack. The ground over which the operation took place was very broken and in parts was unsuitable for tanks. Except for the first two hours of this operation, Lieutenant Karamjeet Singh Judge's platoon was leading in the attack, and up to the last moment Lieutenant Karamjeet Singh Judge dominated the entire battlefield by his numerous and successive acts of superb gallantry.*

Time and again the infantry were held up by heavy medium machine gun and small arms fire from bunkers not seen by the tanks. On every such occasion Lieutenant Karamjeet Singh Judge, without hesitation and with a complete disregard for his own personal safety, coolly went forward through heavy fire to recall the tanks by means of the house telephone. Cover around the tanks was nonexistent, but Lieutenant Karamjeet Singh Judge remained completely regardless not only of the heavy small arms fire directed at him, but also of the extremely heavy shelling directed at the tanks. Lieutenant Karamjeet Singh Judge succeeded in recalling the tanks to deal with bunkers which he personally indicated to the tanks, thus allowing the infantry to advance.

> *In every case Lieutenant Karamjeet Singh Judge personally led the infantry in charges against the bunkers and was invariably first to arrive. In this way ten bunkers were eliminated by this brilliant and courageous officer. On one occasion, while he was going into the attack, two Japanese suddenly rushed at him from a small nullah with fixed bayonets. At a distance of only 10 yards he killed both.*

About fifteen minutes before the battle finished, a last nest of three bunkers was located, which were very difficult for the tanks to approach. An enemy light machine gun was firing from one of them and holding up the advance of the infantry. Undaunted, Lieutenant Karamjeet Singh Judge directed one tank to within 20 yards of the above bunker at great personal risk and then threw a smoke grenade as a means of indication. After some minutes of fire, Lieutenant Karamjeet Singh Judge, using the house telephone again, asked the tank commander to cease fire while he went in with a few men to mop up. He then went forward and got within 10 yards of the bunker, when the enemy light machine gun opened fire again, mortally wounding Lieutenant Karamjeet Singh Judge in the chest. By this time, however, the remaining men of the section were able to storm this strong point, and so complete a long and arduous task.

> *During the battle, Lieutenant Karamjeet Singh Judge showed an example of cool and calculated bravery. In three previous and similar actions this young officer had already proved himself an outstanding leader of matchless courage. In this, his last action, Lieutenant Karamjeet Singh Judge gave a superb example of inspiring leadership and outstanding courage."*

Over time there was a VC presentation ceremony held in India and among the records maintained by the Ministry of Information, in New Delhi is a photograph with the caption, *"Field Marshal Lord Wavell, Viceroy of India presents the VC, to the father of late Lieut. Karamjeet Singh, 15th Punjab Regiment, at a parade held at the Red Fort, on December 19, 1945"*; a copy of that historic photograph was shared with me by Karamjeet's niece, Ms Shah-E-Naaz J Kohli (Boogie to family and friends), the younger daughter of Lieutenant Colonel Ajit Singh Judge.

I was to learn from Boogie that around 1992, Mike Chapman had met her in New Delhi in the course of his research for writing a book on VC recipients and had facilitated her meeting with Major Hugh Baker, in UK. As recalled by Baker, this is how the meeting took place:

"Is that Hugh Baker?"

When I replied "Yes" he went on to say "Did you write a citation for Lieutenant Karamjeet Singh Judge's Victoria Cross in Burma in 1945?" I replied "Yes" again. He then said "I am calling you from New Delhi. Karamjeet's niece is coming to London in a few weeks time and would like to call on you". I replied I would be very pleased to meet her. I was so taken aback I forgot to ask any details, such as her name or where she would be staying in London or a contact telephone number".

Hugh Baker was 80 when Boogie met him and his wife Mable, at their home at Andover (Hants, UK) on October 18, 2000 to hear at first hand the battlefield reminiscences of her uncle, she had never known in life. Baker too had never known Karamjeet till about half an hour before the launch of their mission when they shared cornflake breakfast which for Karamjeet would be the last meal of his heroic, short life. Another significant revelation from that meeting was the fact that for whatever reasons one significant paragraph from Baker's penned citation text was omitted, that is:

"Lieut Karamjeet Singh Judge was undoubtedly the mainstay of the attack and the eyes of the tanks. His men would have been unable to advance on each occasion had he not come forward to bring the tanks back. The crews of the tanks were saved by his example and bravery and they begged of me to write a citation of his deeds".

"I had never met Lieut Karamjeet Singh until a few hours before the attack but I can say without doubt he was the finest leader I ever saw in action. I believe the Myingyan incident will be included in a new book on VCs awarded to Indian soldiers".

It is impossible to reconstruct in words the emotions and bondage of such a meeting but Hugh Baker did leave a brief script of the meeting (he passed away, in 2002) which concludes with this passage from Laurence Binyon's poem, "For The Fallen":

"They shall grow not old,
As we that are left grow old:
Age shall not weary them,
Nor the years condemn.
At the going down of the sun
And in the morning
We will remember them."

Regimental Badge & Shoulder Title of 15 Punjab Regiment in 1945; the crescent moon & Sikh Circlet (Chakri) indicative of mixed caste troops in some units.

Insignia of the Punjab Regiment (left) and Sikh Regiment (Centre) of The Indian Army. Right, Badge of 15th Punjab Regiment, Pak Army.

Karamjeet the college lad, days before enrolment in the Indian Army, 1939.

Ajit Singh Judge enrols in 45 Rattrays Sikhs enroute to entry to OTS, Bangalore.

Brothers Ajit Singh (L) & Karamjeet Singh Judge (R) are commissioned from OTS, Bangalore.

Karamjeet is all smiles, posing for his first portrait as Lieutenant, 1943.

Undaunted, Karamjeet directed one tank to within 20 yards of the bunker at great personal risk, threw a smoke grenade as a means of indication and set about to mop up the remaining nest of bunkers.

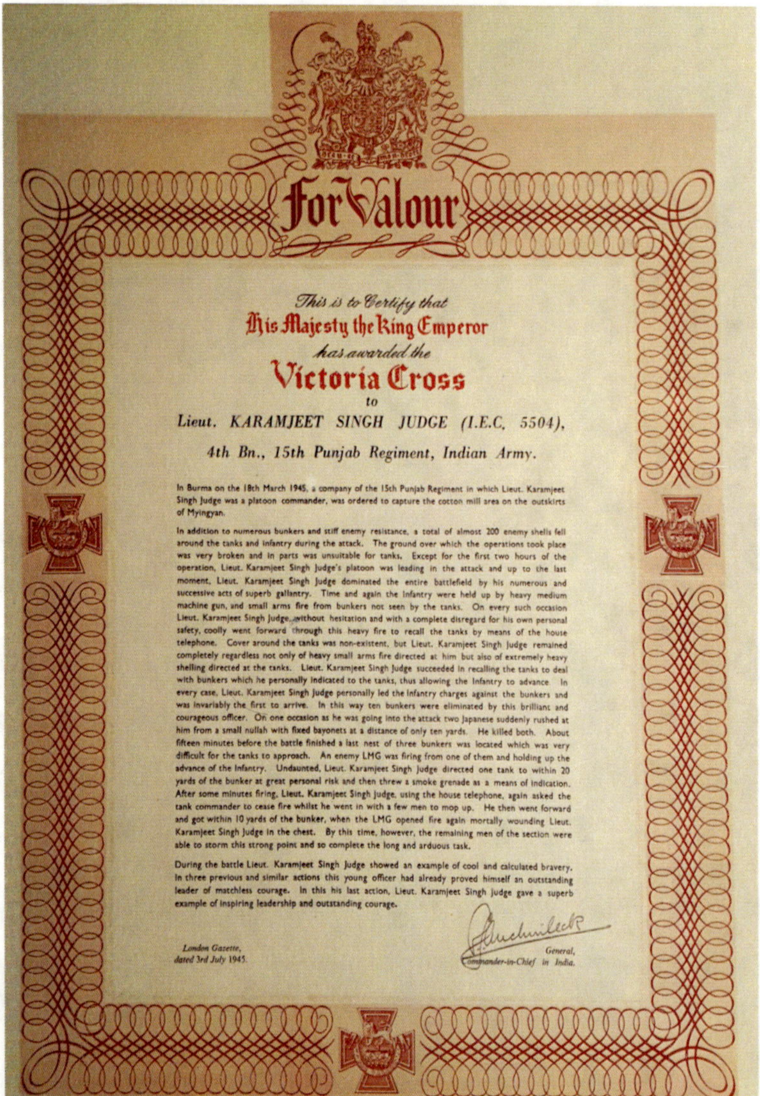

For Valour

This is to Certify that
His Majesty the King Emperor
has awarded the
Victoria Cross
to
Lieut. KARAMJEET SINGH JUDGE (I.E.C. 5504),
4th Bn., 15th Punjab Regiment, Indian Army.

In Burma on the 18th March 1945, a company of the 15th Punjab Regiment in which Lieut. Karamjeet Singh Judge was a platoon commander, was ordered to capture the cotton mill area on the outskirts of Myingyan.

In addition to numerous bunkers and stiff enemy resistance, a total of almost 200 enemy shells fell around the tanks and infantry during the attack. The ground over which the operations took place was very broken and in parts was unsuitable for tanks. Except for the first two hours of the operation, Lieut. Karamjeet Singh Judge's platoon was leading in the attack and up to the last moment. Lieut. Karamjeet Singh Judge dominated the entire battlefield by his numerous and successive acts of superb gallantry. Time and again the Infantry were held up by heavy medium machine gun, and small arms fire from bunkers not seen by the tanks. On every such occasion Lieut. Karamjeet Singh Judge, without hesitation and with a complete disregard for his own personal safety, coolly went forward through this heavy fire to recall the tanks by means of the house telephone. Cover around the tanks was non-existent, but Lieut. Karamjeet Singh Judge remained completely regardless not only of heavy small arms fire directed at him but also of extremely heavy shelling directed at the tanks. Lieut. Karamjeet Singh Judge succeeded in recalling the tanks to deal with bunkers which he personally indicated to the tanks, thus allowing the Infantry to advance. In every case, Lieut. Karamjeet Singh Judge personally led the Infantry charges against the bunkers and was invariably the first to arrive. In this way ten bunkers were eliminated by this brilliant and courageous officer. On one occasion as he was going into the attack two Japanese suddenly rushed at him from a small nullah with fixed bayonets at a distance of only ten yards. He killed both. About fifteen minutes before the battle finished a last nest of three bunkers was located which was very difficult for the tanks to approach. An enemy LMG was firing from one of them and holding up the advance of the Infantry. Undaunted, Lieut. Karamjeet Singh Judge directed one tank to within 20 yards of the bunker at great personal risk and then threw a smoke grenade as a means of indication. After some minutes firing, Lieut. Karamjeet Singh Judge, using the house telephone, again asked the tank commander to cease fire whilst he went in with a few men to mop up. He then went forward and got within 10 yards of the bunker, when the LMG opened fire again mortally wounding Lieut. Karamjeet Singh Judge in the chest. By this time, however, the remaining men of the section were able to storm this strong point and so complete the long and arduous task.

During the battle Lieut. Karamjeet Singh Judge showed an example of cool and calculated bravery. In three previous and similar actions this young officer had already proved himself an outstanding leader of matchless courage. In this his last action, Lieut. Karamjeet Singh Judge gave a superb example of inspiring leadership and outstanding courage.

London Gazette,
dated 3rd July 1945.

Auchinleck
General,
Commander-in-Chief in India.

Lieut Karamjeet Singh's VC citation scroll, signed by Field Marshal Sir Claude Auchinleck, C-in-C in India.

Naik Gian Singh from Karamjeet's Company also took a VC but 14 days earlier and in the same proximity. (Photograph courtesy Sqn Ldr Rana TS Chhina (Retd)).

RETROSPECTIVE

Having uttered on the spur of the moment, *"let us go and get a VC each, Prahji (Brother)"*, shortly, the young lad of seventeen enrols in the Indian Army in 1939, enters Officer Training School, Bangalore in 1942, goes on to become a commissioned officer on May 30,1943, joins his battalion headed for war against the Japanese in Burma, leads his platoon to capture the assigned objective with a mixture of unfaltering determination, inspiring leadership, childlike playfulness yet the ultimate in courage for about twenty five minutes of continuously swift, quick witted and fiercely pitched combat matching in the literal sense the VC Scroll masthead inscription which reads, "For Valour", when on March 18, 1945 that gallant warrior was two months shy of completing twenty one year life span!

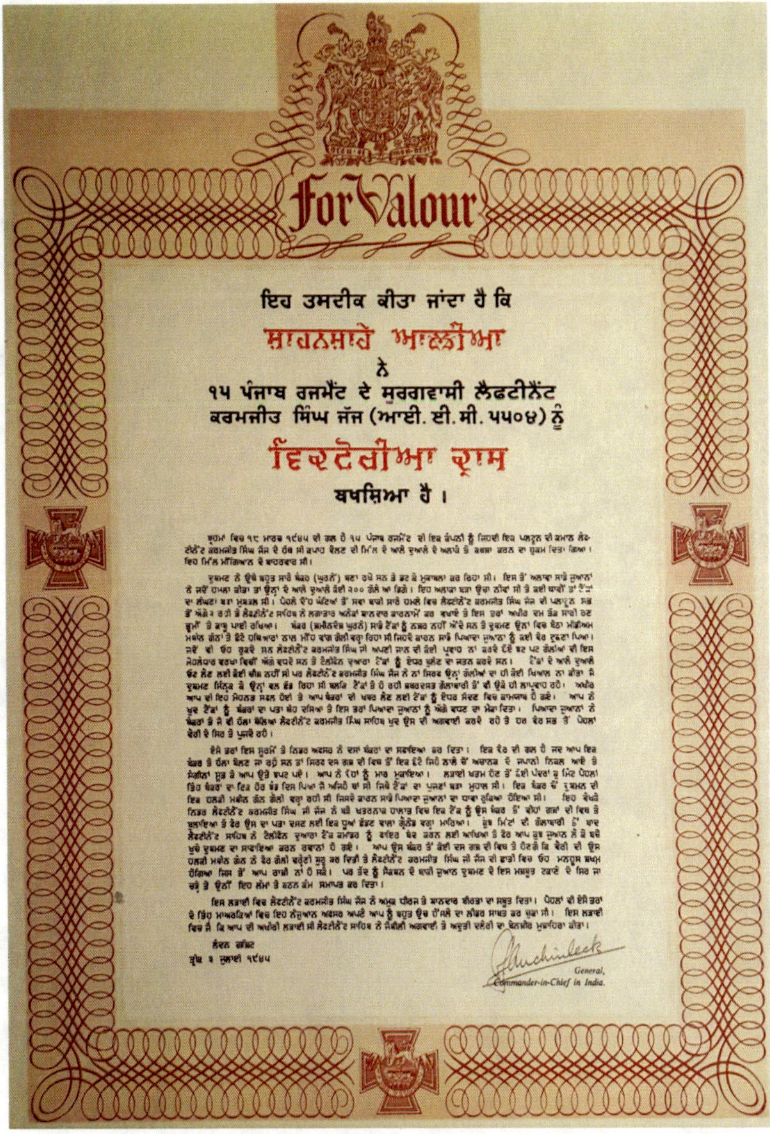

Lieut Karamjeet Singh's VC citation scroll in PUNJABI script, signed by Field Marshal Sir Claude Auchinleck, C-in-C in India.

Sardar Sundar Singh Judge (father of Karamjeet) receives the VC, at Red Fort Delhi from Field Marshal the Lord APJ Wavell, the Viceroy of India.

Karamjeet's VC citation text specifically states the site of battle "ordered to capture Cotton Mills area". Here, the Tayabjis (Indians domiciled in Burma) along with their Burmese friends, the Htoons, are seen having tea in good times, in 1942, in the vicinity of the Cotton Mills. (Photograph courtesy Hashim Tayabji).

Left to Right: Rifleman Bhanbhagta Gurung, VC; Naik Gian Singh, VC; Havildar Umrao Singh, VC.
(Photograph courtesy Punjab State Heroes Memorial, CTB 2016).

RETROSPECTIVE

Having uttered on the spur of the moment, *"let us go and get a VC each, Prahji (Brother)"*, shortly, the young lad of seventeen enrols in the Indian Army in 1939, enters Officer Training School, Bangalore in 1942, goes on to become a commissioned officer on May 30,1943, joins his battalion headed for war against the Japanese in Burma, leads his platoon to capture the assigned objective with a mixture of unfaltering determination, inspiring leadership, childlike playfulness yet the ultimate in courage for about twenty five minutes of continuously swift, quick witted and fiercely pitched combat matching in the literal sense the VC Scroll masthead inscription which reads, "For Valour", when on March 18, 1945 that gallant warrior was two months shy of completing twenty one year life span!

Naik Gian Singh from Karamjeet's Company also took a VC but 14 days earlier and in the same proximity. (Photograph courtesy Sqn Ldr Rana TS Chhina (Retd)).

So there we have perhaps the one and only case from the annals of recorded war histories of the world where a lad makes what would prove to be a prophetic declaration of intent to "get a VC", albeit in innocence, and in less than four years, he does just that! Yet sorrowfully, this is one VC that has ever since remained relegated to pages of war history only and has remained unsung to this day. This aberration in celebratory remembrance at the institutional, regimental and personal levels is sacrilegious to the universally prevalent martial customs, traditions and heritage of the Indian Army; nay the world over.

I was to learn the tale of Karamjeet's VC ambition as also of its intimate links with Smyth's VC related battle scene from WW I, one mid morning in 2008. But the trigger which unfolded this wholesome, episodic war tale (more like a fable) was the sudden surprise and unsavoury move of President Nicolas Sarkozy of France when he banned Sikh students from wearing turbans on the premises of schools and colleges, in France.

As I read the news my thoughts drifted to the history of WW I and of the Indian Army soldiers in thousands who had fought alongside the French Army in the defence of their sovereignty. The thought persisted and I wrote an article titled *"When Sikhs and Turbans Bolstered French Honour"*, pertaining to a valorous battle field action from the Ypres salient, mailed a copy to The Tribune, Chandigarh and another to the Military Attaché at the Embassy of France in New Delhi with a request to forward it to their Hon'ble President. The Tribune was prompt in publishing the article on their OPED page, but I had no response from the French embassy. Be as that may, fortunately, the Government of France did not enforce that turban-ban on the Sikh students in their country.

A most pleasant and completely surprising upshot which followed the publication of my article in The Tribune was an unannounced visit to our home. As I answered the knock on our door, there stood the 88 year old Gentleman Officer, ram rod straight in his immaculate three piece suite (his signature attire), holding out a red rose bud in his left hand as was his wont, whenever he came calling! Lieutenant Colonel Ajit Singh Judge was my first Commanding Officer from way back in 1956 and was to be my icon, all my life.

He was not a frequent visitor but whenever he chose to, he brought laughter, affection and good cheer in our lives always. But that day, he uncharacteristically launched in earnest with the enquiry:

"Baljit, how do you know John Smyth, VC?"

Taken unawares, I was perplexed and reading my unease he brought out the cutting of my article from The Tribune. One thing led to another and by the time we finished lunch I had made a mental note of what has become the main narrative of this slim book, "A Tale of Two Victoria Crosses".

On being commissioned from the Indian Military Academy, Dehra Dun in 1956 I had taken the train to Ferozpur to join my regiment. As customary in those days, I was received by the Senior Subaltern, who over the next few months would be my mentor and guide for regimental history and regimental soldiering. After one week of initiation, he would take me for a "Call" on the Commanding Officer and his lady and caution me on the way to "make polite but brief conversation and only when spoken to. Greet the lady first and the CO thereafter. And under no circumstances must you accept the offer of a second drink. Is that clear, Baljit?"

Seated where I was, up on the facing wall was a VC Scroll in an exquisite gold gilded frame. Beneath the frame was an ornate walnut table and the photograph of a young army officer (almost in his teens), inside a polished silver-plate frame. Torn though I was by curiosity but under the gaze of the Senior Subaltern I could neither get up to read the Scroll nor have a closer look at the portrait of the fellow young officer. Years later, at the first opportunity I spent close to one hour reading the text of that VC Scroll and looking at the framed portrait of the VC recipient, again and again till I could recite the citation and see the portrait even in my sleep.

When Lieutenant Colonel Ajit Singh Judge passed away at the ripe age of 94, I took the liberty of requesting the Colonel's younger daughter (Boogie) for a copy of the Scroll. Being a true chip of the old block, Boogie most generously had an exact replica of the Scroll made true in size and colour tones and gifted to us. In time, my wife and I thought that the Scroll must be given a permanent display in an appropriate Armed Forces establishment, subscribed to by the largest membership of the fraternity. On enquiry from Squadron Leader RTS Chhina, (Secretary, Centre for Armed Forces Historical Research, USI of India, New Delhi) I learnt that the USI did not have any VC Scroll and as such we formalised our choice of the permanent home for it in the USI Library, New Delhi.

At about the same time, my memory drifted to the 1990s when in the course of duty I had visited both the Sikh and Punjab Regimental Centres at Ramgarh (in Jharkhand State) on more than two occasions. On all such visits, it is customary for the hosts to talk about their gallantry decorated, both veterans as also the serving. No matter how hard deep and wide I searched my memory to recall details from that visit but the name Karamjeet would simply not light up in my memory screen.

Why is Karamjeet missing from the Indian Army's regimental history and well entrenched, periodic rituals of honouring the brave hearts? Now at last, I have the probable answer. On termination of WW II, it was natural to downsize the Indian Army to the level relevant for the emerging diktats of perceived external and internal, national security imperatives. Almost concurrently, when India and Pakistan emerged as two sovereign states, the new-look Indian Army was proportionately subdivided between them. In the event, the 4th Battalion of 15 Punjab Regiment was assigned to the Pakistan Army. Much like several other battalions/ regiments, the 4th/15 Punjab had three rifle companies made up of Muslims and one of Jat-Sikhs. In such cases, the agreed protocol for the subdivision of assets provided for the non Muslim caste sub-units to be retained in India and merged with a battalion of similar caste composition.

In the event, the Jat-Sikh company (a.k.a. Karamjeet's Company) of the 4th/15 Punjab remained a part of the Indian Army but despite utmost efforts, I was unable to find evidence of its post August 1947, regimental new identity. However, there are strong leads to suggest that it was merged with the Sikh Regiment of the Indian Army because Captain Isher Singh, VC, Major Prakash Singh, VC and Naik Gian Singh, VC were all from one of the Punjab group of battalions/regiments but following the Partition of India we find them all taken on the rolls of the Sikh Regiment. As a matter of fact, Naik Gian Singh's VC citation reveals that he had emerged in the forefront of a death defying action on March 02, 1945 that is exactly 16 days prior to Karamjeet's VC feat and in the same general area of Myingyan-Cotton Mills during the same ongoing mission to enlarge and secure the firm base, for the capture of Meiktila. More than that, Naik Gian Singh at that time was also serving in Karamjeet's rifle Company *per se*. But post August 1947, the 5 Sikh Battalion would thenceforth be Naik Gian Singh's new kinsmen. So by inference, Karamjeet's VC legacy must presently belong to both the Sikh and Punjab Regiments of the Indian Army and at the combat formation level, Karamjeet may well be a glorious motivational fulcrum for the 7 Infantry Division, just as well.

Be as that may, much of the recorded regimental history pertaining to Karamjeet's Company and deeds of its individuals got wiped out in the process of the subdivision of the erstwhile monolithic Indian Army and Karamjeet remains confined, almost entirely to the pages of VC history. The 4th/15 Punjab got re-designated in the Pakistan Army as 12 Punjab but because of the mutual and persistent acrimony between the two neighbouring nations, Karamjeet's VC became a mere statistic. Hopefully, this slim book will reinstate Lieutenant Karamjeet Singh Judge, VC in the war history, battle remembrance celebrations and motivation halls of both the Sikh and Punjab Regiments as also among the Indian Army, at large. And in the spirit of the universal brotherhood of veteran brave hearts, Karamjeet's VC legacy is there as much to be cherished by the 12 Punjab of Pakistan Army, (the avatars of the 4th/15 Punjab of 1947) because battle field valour transcends boundaries of friend and foe.

As of now, we may take comfort that the names of Gian Singh and Karamjeet will be celebrated and remembered in perpetuity as they lie engraved on the same VC panel of the marble dome over the "Memorial Pavilion" in the complex of "The Memorial Gates War Memorial", located in Hyde Park Corner, in London. And by a strange but fortuitous coincidence, engraved on the adjoining right hand panel is the name of JG Smyth, the inspiration and icon of Karamjeet!

The memorial complex was inaugurated by Her Majesty Queen Elizabeth II in 2002 where the inscription reads:

"In memory of the 5 million volunteers from the Indian Subcontinent, Africa and the Caribbean who fought with Britain in the two World Wars".

More prominent is another inscription credited to the writer Ben Okri on the Pillars of the entry gates thus:

"Our Future Is Greater Than Our Past".

As for my one other memorable link to Karamjeet, it takes me back to my school days in the 1940s. Major TM Whitmarsh-Knight (known to friends as Johnny and to the family as Tubby) was a young Cambridge Don at the time of his enlistment for war service. Tubby too had taken a bullet or two in his abdomen but survived to ripe old age. Now in 1948, Tubby returned to India to take up appointment as the Senior Master at the Bishop Cotton School, Simla and he taught me English language, English literature and Indian History (Mughal period) and was pleased with my performance in the School Leaving, Senior Cambridge University Examination in December, 1952. In a residential Public School, it was not unusual for teachers to develop close bonds with their wards especially in those days when each class had no more than twenty students. And Mr Knight had often regaled us with his experiences from WW II.

On more than one occasion, during the monthly informal visit to the Senior Master's Lodge, I had heard Mr Knight narrating the exceptional courageous action of his platoon officer, Karamjeet Singh with feelings of profound admiration for that young lad's sense of duty. In hindsight, I believe that was Tubby's "punch line" for motivating and inculcating among all of us the ideals of committed citizens of India. Tubby had known that I was headed for a life in the Indian Army but who could have guessed that five years later, within days after graduation from the Indian Military Academy, Dehra Dun that when taken to "Call" on my Commanding Officer in an army bungalow in the shadow of a Memorial to War Heroes (Saragarhi Gurdwara Sahib at Ferozepur), I would be seated facing Karamjeet's VC Scroll and his portrait!

As we know by now, Boogie had gone to UK in mid October, 2000 explicitly to meet Hugh Baker who was the sole surviving witness of the entire 35 minute long combat mission of Karamjeet's platoon for the capture of the Cotton Mills area (Myingyan) on 18 March, 1945. On November 02, 2000 Hugh Baker wrote a letter thanking Boogie for visiting them and once again reminisced about Karamjeet's fearless leadership in face of awesome odds thus:

"After eliminating ten enemy bunkers, he (Sic. Karamjeet) directed one tank to within 20 yards of another bunker and asked the tank commander to cease-fire once he went in to mop up. While doing so he was mortally wounded… I was so mad at the enemy machine gunner that killed Karamjeet that instead of destroying the bunker with my 75 mm gun (which I could not lower as by now I was too near to it) I ran the tank over it several times reducing the bunker to rubble...

I wrote the citation on 20 March, free hand on the normal Army Signal Message Pad… Even though I am 82 years old, I can still vividly remember that action as though it was yesterday."

I was curious to learn the details about Hugh Baker's MC, and so mailed a request to his son Max Baker for a copy of the MC citation. Unfortunately, due to an upheaval in his domestic life, he was unable to access his old possessions but confirmed that Hugh's tank troop was in the lead of what, after the capture of Meiktila, came to be called "The race for Rangoon".

But what amused me was a peephole insight into the cantonment life in India's hinterland during the preparatory phase of Field Marshal Slim's Burma Campaign. Hugh Baker's 116 Regiment (Gordon Highlanders), Royal Armoured Corps happened to be garrisoned at Hyderabad and Hugh was obviously a charming subaltern of refined and cultured manners and spent evenings amidst the charmed circles of Hyderabad's socialite elites. So much so that he became the indispensable Bridge partner of none other than the

Nawab of Hyderabad! And this is what his son narrated in his mail of 04 November, 2012:

"Dear Baljit,

When Dad was in India he was friends with the Nizam and used to be picked up in the evenings to play Bridge with him. One of the Nizam's friends which he (the Nizam) wanted to marry him off to, was called Frenni Homogi (Not sure of the spelling) and the Nizam offered my Dad a commission in the Deccan Horse and a salary of 20,000 Rupees a month. But Dad was already engaged to my mum and was sent in the advance party to Burma to avoid a diplomatic incident.

My Dad often wondered what happened to her and he did meet someone who went to her wedding after the war.

Just a wild request but you never know

regards

Max

PS: I'll try and find the MC and MBE citations.

PPS: I heard from Boogie after a few years. Must reply."

**Going by the Parsi community's family surnames lexicon, I presume the last name of the maiden was Homji?*

I need hardly state that the Nizam of Hyderabad's Deccan Horse is one among the present day Indian Army's proud and battle hardened regiments with lofty war record. But fancy the Nawab's offer of Rs 20,000 monthly salary to entice Hugh Baker to a future which held out all the elements of an oriental romance! But then Gentlemen Officers are made of sterner metal and Hugh was a gallant man to have remained true to his fiancée.

Having concluded this narrative, I was absorbed by the thought that in fact I did have a copy (possibly, kind courtesy the Centre for Armed Forces Historical Research, USI of India, New Delhi) of the MC citation which Hugh Baker's Commanding Officer had initiated from the war zone, a few months before the end of WW II. But it would take me an agonising two weeks before I reset my eyes upon it. And what a war booty at that, as it bears recommendations up the chain of command with signatures of the brilliant IV Corps Commander, Lieutenant General FW Messervy and finally of that Warlord, Field Marshal WJ Slim, Commander Allied Land Forces, South East Asia Command, signed on 31 August, 1945.

And this is how it reads:

"Captain H Baker, 116 Regiment (Gordons) R.A.C., has commanded a troop in operations since 10 February, 1945. He has been engaged in forty five actions. This officer has shown keenness in his desire to close with the enemy, and many actions have been brought to a successful conclusion through his forcefulness and initiative. He has at all times displayed the highest qualities of leadership. At Nyakaing in cooperation with 2 K. O. S. B., his troop, by moving to the rear of the village, accounted for forty two of the enemy who would otherwise have escaped and during the operations to clear Myingyan his troop, unsupported, cleared the Northern

portion of the town, continuing the action until darkness and the retreat of the enemy left the area completely in our hands."

Sd: JWF BLACKATOR
Lt Col
O.C. 116 Regt (Gordon Highlanders) R.A.C.
15 May, 1945.

It is natural and even understandable that military narratives would confine to soldiers, their deeds in victory and defeat and sites of battle encounters. But except for the accounts of battles in Europe, the accounts of sorrows and sufferings of the inhabitants which are perhaps the ugliest manifestation of any war are, by and large seldom recounted. So, in the instant case of the Cotton Mills battle site, when about a decade ago a manuscript narrative of the war in Burma written by one Tyabji was shared with me (for reading only and return) by Aasheesh Pittie, a friend, it provided me the uncommon opportunity to link the experiences of a victim of that war with the texts of battles fought in Burma, both in 1942 and again in 1944-45.

The Tyabjis' were one among several prominent families of India with well established commercial interests of long standing and living as domiciles in Burma. Presently, almost all of them were among the huge exodus set on their way for refuge in India, following the Japanese invasion of Burma. Many had perished en-route due to sheer fatigue, starvation and sickness and less than half survived the ordeal. The Tyabjis were among the lucky survivors mostly because they had possessions with which to acquire advantage for safe passage to the Indian hinterland. But they were also magnanimous by way of using their wealth to provide succour to the less privileged fellow refugees, fleeing Burma for sanctuary in India.

I had perhaps exceeded my brief by retaining a copy of one B & W photograph from that manuscript, of the Tyabjis on a stop-over at Magwe (due South but not far from the Cotton Mills battle site), midway to their primary staging destination at Mandalay. Their grandson Hashim most graciously put names to the personalities through the mail below:

Dear Sir,

Yes I can indeed identify the people in the photograph.

From Left to Right: SAS Tyabji (my Grandfather); Akhtar Tyabji (Grandmother); Mr. Kya Htoon (close friend of grandparents. He was a lawyer and a Karen); Mrs. Kya Htoon; Miss. Olga Kya Htoon. I would be interested to know how you got this picture. I have it with me and my father's note says it was taken in Magwe on 11th March 1942 after Rangoon had fallen. Shortly after this picture was taken (if the date on it is correct) everyone in it moved to Mandalay. SAS Tyabji had been given the honorary rank of Lt. Col in the Indian Army and had organised a mobile rice mill carried on 30 trucks with 50 truck loads of paddy to supply the Army and refugee columns using the northern route.

I have to say though that I have my suspicions that the date on the photograph could be wrong.

kind regards

Hashim

Dated, 13 March, 2017.

Despite the remarkable fortitude of the Tyabji family and friends in the face of dire circumstances, the photograph will remain a harsh reminder of the futility of war; deaths and dislocations of innocent countless and nameless people from their homes and hearths and concurrently, thousands of soldiers lives given to reclaim what was the real estate but in the process reduced to utter rubble.

May be it is time for mankind to step back and simply contemplate the wisdom of the verse from "The Battle of Blenheim" which must surely confront the conscience of all societies:

"Now tell us all about the War,
And what they fought each other for?"

Entrance to the Memorial Gates Complex, on the Constitution Hill, London.

The Memorial Pavilion Dome on the Constitution Hill, London.

In the interior of the Pavilion Dome are inscribed the names of all the VC recipients.

The VC Memorial Pavilion in London providentially showcases both brave hearts; Karamjeet up front and Smyth 2nd on right-hand panel. Naik Gian Singh's name is way above Karamjeet's, that is third from top. Also inscribed is Ganju Lama, the one and only Sikkimese (of Tibetan descent) to win gallantry recognition in WW II.

The Memorial Gates

The Memorial Gates

The uplifting Quote (from the novelist Ben Okri) on the Pillars of the Memorial Gates, London.

Ajit Singh Judge (impeccably dressed as always) Commanding 5 Bombay Mountain Battery in J&K, in 1949. The 5 Bombay Mountain Battery were raised in 1827 and are the proud, senior-most Gunner unit of the Indian Artillery.

Lieutenant Colonel Ajit Singh Judge, at his 88th birthday bash! By my reckoning, unarguably the best dressed Gentleman Officer. He took premature retirement in 1964 to become the Founder CEO of the Coco Cola Bottling Plant at Chandigarh (a family inheritance of Mrs Surinder Judge)

The suave Lieut Hugh Baker (Bridge playing partner of none less than the Nizam of Hyderabad); he was witness to Karamjeet's heroic deeds from close proximity & wrote the VC (Posthumous) citation. (Photograph courtesy Max Baker).

Lieut Colonel Ajit Singh's daughter (Boogie) traces out Maj Hugh Baker in 2000, in UK, for a first hand account of Karamjeet's valorous deed.

Maj Hugh Baker, MC at a reunion dinner in 1998 with Maj Gen Sir Evelyn John Webb-Carter. His son Max is in the middle. (Photograph courtesy Max Baker).

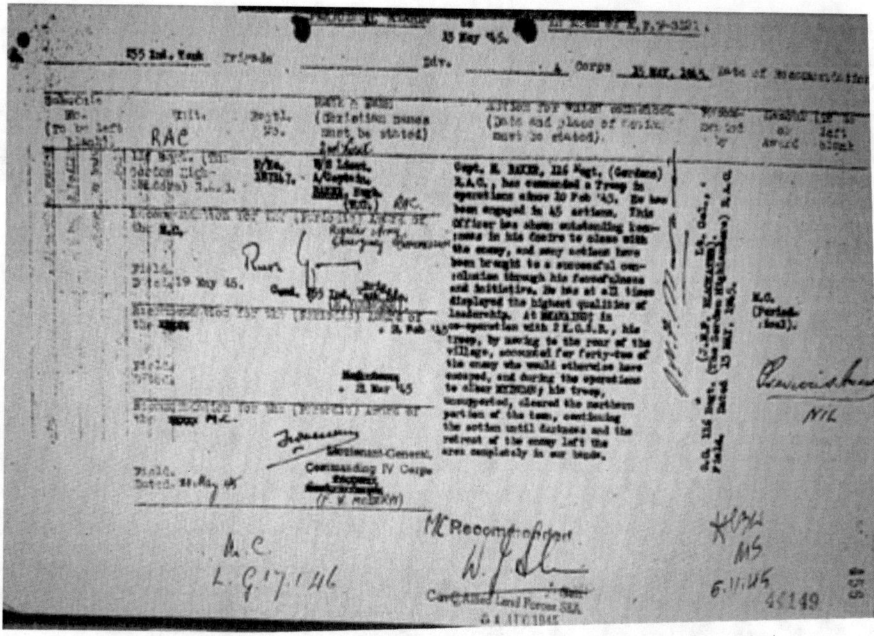

Capt. H. BAKER, 116 Regt. (Gordons) R.A.C., has commanded a Troop in operations since 20 Feb '45. He has been engaged in 45 actions. This Officer has shown outstanding keenness in his desire to close with the enemy, and many actions have been brought to a successful conclusion through his forcefulness and initiative. He has at all times displayed the highest qualities of leadership. At [illegible] in co-operation with 2 K.O.S.B., his troop, by moving to the rear of the village, accounted for forty-two of the enemy who would otherwise have escaped, and during the operations to clear [illegible], his troop, unsupported, cleared the northern portion of the town, continuing the action until darkness and the retreat of the enemy left the area completely in our hands.

MC Citation for Capt Hugh Baker initiated by his Commanding Officer, on 15 May, 1945 & processed all the way to Field Marshal WJ Slim, 31 August, 1945.

Mr TM Whitmarsh-Knight (Karamjeet's Company Commander), now Senior Master Bishop Cotton School, Simla), also doubled as House Master, Rivaz House; seated in middle, 1950. YS Nakai on his Right, became IG Police, Haryana.

A rare bunch of brave hearts; Capt Ishar Singh VC, Sub Karam Singh PVC, Maj Prakash Singh VC & Capt Gian Singh VC; all from the SIKH Regiment post August, 1947 (photograph courtesy the Punjab State Heroes Memorial, CTB 2016).

EPILOGUE

This Book is humbly published for the reinstatement of Lieutenant Karamjeet Singh Judge, VC (Posthumous) among the pantheon of War Heroes of both the

Indian Army's Punjab & Sikh Regiments

And

12 Punjab, Pakistan Army.

Because, the brotherhood of War Heroes belong to all mankind, in equal measure.

R I P Karamjeet

The Tankkyan Cremation Memorial in Myanmar where Lieutenant Karamjeet Singh Judge "is commemorated along with all men (that is, 1060 commemorations, 981 Indians) of the Forces of undivided India and the Army of Burma who died during the 1939-1945 World War and whose mortal remains were accorded the last rites required by their religion – committed to fire".